AT THIEVERY END

An Anthology

RAND LEEB-DU TOIT

EXO scalr
HOUSE

AT THIEVERY END

EXOscalr House

a division of EXOscalr Pty Limited

Sydney, Australia

ISBN: 978-0-6480807-3-2

For my wife, Beryl,
who has been with me
through apartheid and the
coronavirus pandemic.

everything is closed
you are open
the world lies
paused and unfinished
you complete me

Preface

An anthology of poems bookended by human tragedy.

Initially written over 25 years ago during the apartheid era while serving as an unwilling conscript in the South African Defence Force and recently updated during the global pandemic.

These poems are presented as a unique slant on life in and beyond the global pandemic.

Stay forever hopeful.

the portals of my mind house this dream that pigments my imag-
ination
    it is i who creates the battle as time bears no conscience
    let me alone or allow me to tear down the walls protecting my
sanity
    mirrors hold no truths and too the sand lies thick upon the hour
glass
    yet it is me i look down upon from my hovering amidst the
clouds of realism
    i am impartial to the weight i shoulder yet the ball and chain
drag deep

hold me close against your body and tear me from this nightmare
    prepare me slowly
    ferment my strength
    and when the day comes
    let me breathe like a good wine
    then you and the world can only be mine

- *the countdown*

when i lie awake at night thinking of thee
    my body is asleep but my mind is free
    i caress thine sacred places with my immense thoughts
    oh, if only thou wert with me

during my drought when i must be alone
    i carry out my work with mechanical vigour
    i let my mind dwell on thy body and succour
    oh, i will thee to be mine and to take my throne

- *missing you*

fluorescence glorifies her epitome
    defying gravity defying all laws
    hanging like an ogre
    miniature utility
    darkness envelopes the wall
    her claws
    feeling the electrifying pulse in the air
    she listens in to the zoom call
    standing alone
    seeing all with revolving eyes
    a rotating stare
    lying flat to the wall
    wings of a pair
    suffering for her ugliness
    stereotypes to pity
    sophisticated by nature
    influenced by the mean
    the frail forgotten fly clings to the wall
    impurity she is ready to move on
    to become part of another scene

- looking on

an eagle gliding the crystal bronze
 doves performing the art of love
 a yacht cruising the caribbean
 waves attacking living coal reef
 of these things man is fond
 peace and tranquility
 a shore break devouring virgin sands
 puppets clinging to rock face
 a toy boat idling in the eye of hurricane
 women's thighs dripping sex
 of these things man is fond
 adrenaline pumping
 where has man's utopia drifted
 lost in a city's back streets.

- for rodriguez

when a place
    slides into
    the recesses
    of our minds
    it becomes
    but a flash
    a glimpse of
    an earlier
    existence that
    now lurks like
    a predator
    on the fringe
    of a herd
    waiting to
    attack at
    the slightest
    sign of
    weakening

and so it
    is at what
    feels like the
    end of the
    world
    butterflies flit
    across the
    surface while
    monsters lurk
    in the deep
    pools surfacing
    inopportunely

to remind
one of a
place once
called home

- far from home

above the populous
    of the square
    i sit and watch
    the tourists haughty
    high heel
    click clacking
    cobblestones
    while in the cabinets
    of the young old man
    the watches won't wind
    from my window
    this world turns
    slowly round
    and round
    a right
    merry-go-round
    of culture
    while in the corner
    sun beats down
    on the bald brown beggar
    this morning
    i descended onto
    the square and sat alone
    the cobblestones
    are cold and damp
    the beggar
    huddled in the rain
    the stalls are memories of summer
    long ago

- sitting in on the square

eyes darting to and fro
    nervous comprehension
    strange faces leering back
    moguls out of a dark dream
    new tastes new smells new sounds
    stirring up the tension
    figures without form
    dust is the norm
    coffee without cream
    is it real
    is he really here
    so many things
    so unclear

time passes see
    the sun rise and
    see it set
    new day new life
    no colour

a secret society
    men without mind
    boys stepping on
    the stones of time – strife
    ice cold dawn
    hot is the norm
    so different yet
    so little variety
    what is happening in the real world
    does she still love him

he has nothing to fear

- *stones of time*

you are a
    wilted flower
    your petals
    dried out
    cracked and
    scarred your leaves
    wince with every
    breath of
    wind
    the sun which
    once gave your energy
    is now your
    enemy
    it drains your
    substance away
    and leaves you
    frail
    you will die
    soon and return
    all that you
    stole from
    the earth
    even your memories
    will dissolve into
    the cauldron
    of time
    for none shall
    remember

your face is hidden
    behind a mask

of painted clay
yet even that
is etched in pain
while through the cracks
wrinkles creep
the skin which once
was savored
has lost its colour
blotches mark your body
and sores fester
they will not heal
because they realise
there is no use
time has caught
you up
and will win
the race
for none shall
remember

- ode to an aged care resident

living in a world of his own
    johannes grunts his emotions at the sea
    mute the wind tousles his hair
    unkempt like his mind
    his back slightly bent under
    the weight of the sun
    which engrains its tracks
    on a face lined
    with laughter at our
    world in crows feet of
    loneliness and pain
    while bright blue eyes
    mirror his playmates
    the hissing ocean
    and the silent sky
    yet behind these
    sparkling portals a
    dark grey void lingers
    as he combs the beaches
    like I comb his mind

- beach runner

ITS BEAT
>fast slow fast
>live at your own speed
>be dictated to by no man
>live by your own creed
>let only the word of
>the one shape your deeds

ITS FLOW
>rejoice when you are happy
>weep when you are sad
>know your moods
>identify your feelings
>for you are an individual
>born alone
>you will die alone
>but do not be selfish
>apply your knowledge
>to the benefit of all
>let others learn from you
>criticise and accept criticism but
>always adapt in the light
>of what you discover
>in your travels

ITS PATH
>sail the seas in search of answers
>the questions are inside you
>manifesting themselves and coagulating
>into a thick mass of confusion
>but somewhere along the route you travel

the catalyst will be added
you will light up and
the whole world will begin to fall
under the eye of eternity

ITS MESSAGE
the crystal waters will
reflect your image
like a mirror
you will see the light
living is good but
dying will be better
if you live right
your life will float
under your nose
like a waft of sage
you will be at one with
the rhythm of life

the gravel
    soothes
    my aching mind
    bitter-sweet
    the taste lingers
    in my throat
    look at me
    little ones and
    think me unkind
    am i
    the one they
    will label scapegoat?

the wintry sun
    blazes down on
    a pallid landscape
    a finger of acrid
    yellow smoke
    probes the sky
    so many friends i
    have lost so many
    enemies I will make
    all is quiet
    on the internal front
    i wonder why?

fostered in them I sense
    a culpable ignorance
    a foolish calm
    i myself have darker fears
    more dire visions

of the future
let them live in
their cocoons of power
let them come to harm
should these acts
of self – preservation
be allowed to nurture?

where do we go to
my lovely, the time
draws so near
this land that
looks as ravaged
as a tired whore
please pray
for peace but don't
waste a tear
the cauldron
of covidia , can it
crack anymore?

- *the cauldron*

he spoke to me in that familiar drone
 it was like a drug now
 i was dependent on him for support
 the buzz of his voice relaxing me
 easing the pain of my realisation
 the little man inside my head
 finally told me the stark truth

- you are insane

whale
    gargantuan mammal
    ruler of oceans
    oh my friend!
    white washed by man and time
    bones on the sand
    graveyard to man's achievements
    mother nature's wonder turned into soap
    to do this?

whale
    solitary spout
    rare excitement
    i see you!
    glistening silver black against your spray
    a living oil tanker - fuelled for extinction
    dive submarine dive - you are innocent to your fate
    as i am innocent to mine.

- mirror

what images you
    conjure
    in your mind
    images of youth
    idealistic truths
    nurture
    until the day
    you join
    the real world
    in the games
    they play

so for now
    keep up that
    precious smile
    remembering
    the truth
    is never far
    from fiction

- from behind a pane of glass

15

coke cakes
　　grass grows
　　man withers
　　god knows

- *cycle of life*

to bring a child
    onto the wheel
    to watch it
    roll over crushing
    life from one's blood

to escape
    to an untouched island
    to soak up peace
    watching mushroom clouds
    mar the horizon

bleaker prospects I know not
    for the future
    holds no shining light

oppose parental instincts
    forget the sounds of playful youth
    every child has the right
    to remain uncreated

- birth right

a painting
    hanging on a wall
    in the hall
    eyes piercing
    peering at us
    leering from the shadows
    a painting hanging on the
    opposite wall
    in the hall

- lockdown. surreal segregation

the great bull wasps his tail
    through the midday haze
    rupturing his immutable complacency
    for your congealed colonial beak
    while his shot eyes flicker wildly
    and he sends a rumble through his folds
    which have shrunk
    under your growing weight

you render him free of mindless parasites
    or so you say
    but the ooze that flows is his
    you are the parasite my friend

and now he awakens
    from his mid-day slumber
    beware he sees the danger
    but he smells blood his blood
    he hears hungry rumblings
    his deeper than yours

thunder is edging closer
    signalling an early close
    to this lazy afternoon
    lightning will fork
    you from his back
    and it will be night

the system
    hangs hazy
    over your head
    establishment blues swing lazily
    through the sky
    some say some
    say you are dead
    we never can
    tell we know
    you cannot die

sing me your song
    sugar man, star
    man, any man
    cranium commands
    defying body urge the good
    seducing the bad
    producing the ugly
    listen to me
    hear my blood
    curdle - hear my dream

i bring to society
    my declaration
    of insanity talking
    to the little man
    reality rushes by
    people places prerogatives
    rhythmic murmurs
    of a better time
    eternal in

the infinity
of the cosmos
we wait for the correct
puzzle - self destruct
to you I bring
the wrong for you
this sad song
tell me all
tell me all
what appall

torn between two worlds
    i stand, devastated
    by the forbidden
    cell of humankind
    sick is how I feel
    when my thoughts formulate
    this prison
    too long we strut
    through the rut hanging
    our heads in shame
    for you are not innocent
    double standards
    in the games
    we play don't
    cheat yourself my friend
    for you have set
    your own trap
    follow in my footsteps
    and be careful
    not to shuffle
    their eyes will torment
    you and suck your thoughts
    into their void

look at their sun
    how it lights up your tunnel
    the wind streams
    back your resistance
    and contaminates your mind
    feel free to do exactly
    what you want but

remember not to break
their rules and regulations
sing my song of hate
for their system society
for the dead of spirit
you walk through their midst
flow with their stream
for someday
you will swim away
from their current
and you too will climb
the banks of sanity

- undertones in the flow

fragile toothpick
    wearing running
    shoes – grotesque
    sight wading through
    swirling eddies
    her mechanism
    slowly grinding
    to a halt

- old woman crossing city street

red lines of vision
    splitting
    an open blade
    of grass
    tainted verges
    on a sea
    of darkness
    with a bright throbbing orb
    hanging
    amongst its waves

clinical oxygen curling
    into
    my nostrils
    coagulating
    in my throat
    as a thick phlegm
    and reemerging
    in a
    burst
    of hot breath

sounds to curdle what
    little blood
    is left
    scalpels tinkling
    fast hoarse groans
    the creaking
    of a bed
    nurses tittering
    amidst the tension

the acrid dryness
    of cleanliness
    anaesthetised
    nicotine lingering
    with the
    undissolved powder
    of a tablet
    seepages mixed with
    cracked dry blood
    on my lips

i lie propped up
    in bed and wait.

when i look through the window
   i see a solitary cloud
   and i wonder to where do you go?

when i lie on my back and look into the night sky
   i see the milky way
   and i wonder how high do you fly?

when i skip from rock to rock
   i see a pair of eagles
   and i wonder to where do you flock?

when i look in the mirror
   i see a thousand faces
   and i wonder to where do you go

where are your chosen places?

to chip a brick in the wall
    to make a young man fall
    it is so easy to dislodge time
    it is so simple to dismember a mind
    break down my hopes cut down the ropes
    my bridge is sliding away
    cross me today

- fragile mind

if the sky were blue and i fell in love with you
    could we sail across an azure sky
    could we forget to ask the old ones why?

if the birds still sang and the church bells rang
    would there be an international amnesty
    would we answer our children honestly?

if any member of the family should decease
    from the shelter you must release
    for the fear of contamination
    lies heavier than trump's damnation

- children of the aftermath

to sink to such levels of pain
    and then to soar beyond ecstasy
    horrendous in its shape my leg
    dissolving before my very eyes

pig eyes of death unblinking
    as she cruised below me unsuspecting
    her dorsal fin breaking the surface
    as she lined up her prey

i saw her when she dived
    big grey mother of a beast
    hitting me hard with the momentum
    of all five metres of her length

the dream broke suddenly unfortunately
    realisation of billowing clouds of red
    obscuring the coral below
    my blood ebbing slowly and dissipating

what a wonderful day it had been
    scrambling for my surfboard
    i recall my lady lying on the beach
    she is coming at me again.

the sun bursts forth with new found power
    ice and snow it quickly dissolves
    freeing the waters of swamp and of river
    of lake and of sea
    to leap and to sparkle in their new found liberty

bright sun shining across the full blue sky
    the winter and abdominal cold recede
    sun looks down with an unclouded face
    snow melts away with elegant grace
    faces of men beam like one
    icicles give way with a deep sounding sigh

rain falling from a sad sky
    people sitting heaving a sigh
    nothing to do nowhere to go
    day drags on time too slow

clouds crossing an azure sky
    people moving feeling fine
    so much to do so little time
    day almost gone sun too high

- *time*

i read and it was there
    i looked and they were bared
    i talked and they just stared

- *sex is everywhere*

take a walk through
    an open field
    put on a set
    of blinkers and
    imagine that you
    are totally alone
    there are no signs
    of the civilisation
    that places you under
    its stranglehold

then when you have
    relaxed its pull on you
    try to feel what
    it would be like
    to live on an
    unchanging world
    a world of permanent fixtures
    rigid standards and
    unbending principles
    where the forces of
    nature rule by day
    and by night
    the only sights
    smells and sounds are
    from the beginning
    of time

let the freedom of
    such a place take
    a hold on your

inner soul
allow your senses
to soar outwards
and then remember
that you are in
one small field and
that maybe maybe
one day we will
not need to
put on a set
of blinkers and
imagine

what shall we say
    to one another
    upon the death
    of a brother

shall we offer
    condolences and
    shed the odd tear

or will we sink
    to a lower
    level than his
    killers and cower

- on the death of a fellow struggler

living under the weight of the world
    burdened by their dream-images
    soft borderline appearances flitter
    across their eyelids at the point of
    waking and of falling asleep.
    they have never seen moons float through
    ponds of silver flecked lilies
    nor do they know the joy of idle
    chatter as the sun heaves itself through
    the midday high.
    behind them burns the fire of their souls
    while a raised wall separates them
    from the warmth and colour of reality
    and above this wall great statues are
    paraded endlessly

a little village of sun baked huts made
    of clay and straw nestled
    high amidst the mountains of our wilderness
    they know not of politics of hustle and bustle
    yet they are content

the prisoners face their cave wall and
    cannot see one another nor objects
    behind them placed above the wall
    and although they are being punished for
    the morality of their forefathers
    to live their lives seeing only shadows
    of reality and to hear only echoes
    off the wall they cling to familiar

shadows their passions and prejudices
if they were freed from their bondages to
turn around and see the realities
which produce their fantasies they would
be blinded by the light of their fires
they would become angry and
prefer to regain their shadow-world

the village cordoned off
from society by a ring of steel
from the hill they see the
valley of green the valley that
produces their darkness
murmurings of discontent rumble
amidst their shadows
as they prepare to break the chains
of their bondings

but if only one prisoner was freed
from their chains and allowed to see to
really see all around them in the cave
the firelight their fellow prisoners
and then to drag themselves out
into the sun so they see the world
the world in all her splendour no shadows
no optical and political illusions
their ideals would change and they would dream
in reflections and after images no longer
and yet if they were to descend back
into the cave they would have difficulty
the darkness would envelop them totally
they would become subject to their peers'
ridicule scorn even to physical attack

for us the current flickerings

on the wall must be recognised
and overcome to give us new hope
a new feeling of reality
and to throw away our old conjectures.

- *the cave*

shovelled in
    shovelled out
    like dirt - my
    memories cling
    to a time
    before all this
    bitterness
    questions linger
    amidst the smoke
    of a conscience
    billowing
    dark against
    the stark
    nakedness
    of a soul
    lost in time

get a job, boy!
    just something
    to keep
    you going
    to keep
    the hunger
    pains at bay
    whilst your brain
    strains
    to grip
    the reality
    of the system
    that

has already
dug your grave
amongst
the rocks
of your race

yet the pain
marks remain
alongside
the wrinkles
of my smile
at the absolute
futility
of a comic
creed
whose justice
sparks deep

my stomach
grumbles
as the storm
clouds roll
over the country
i should call
mine
still - life
goes on
for the privileged
cringing lower
in the safety
of their
suburbs

will
they

swallow me
into their
fetid
system?

34

---

always better than the best
    motto of a madman - motto of a fool
    how many people - how many minds
    oblivious to the world in its ecosystem

uniformity leads to teamwork
    broken like a porcelain doll
    built into a transparent brick wall
    living on the edge in their mould

communication leads to efficiency
    drifting aimlessly - waiting for instructions
    hurry up and wait the watchwords
    smoke sifting through a winter sky - blown away

the soldier green as a shoot ready to be shot
    the nurse exhausted but ready for the shift

i'm sitting here waiting
　i'm sitting here anticipating
　how long has it been
　how long will it be

time has gone so slow yet so fast
　i have been wearing a painted mask
　people passing in the street nearly knock me off my feet
　living in a timepiece life is no treat

i'm sitting here waiting
　i'm sitting here anticipating
　can you still want me
　can it still be love

my mind swirls around in space
　around you it makes its base
　i just take up my pen
　until I see you again until I see you again

- *waiting*

like a pair of pure white doves we sit
   the rope is slack but the knot is tied
   away we must fly and for a time cannot sit
   the rope is taut and the knot it tied
   time passes
   the rope lengthens
   the knot becomes tighter
   soon we will be together again
   the rope will become slack but
   the knot will remain tight

- *love knot*

another long day another long day
    i wish i could be so far away
    i wonder if the sun will rise
    i see shadows in their guise
    another long day another long day
    for you for how long must I pray

- patience

in these hard times
    long must we wait
    our feelings are known
    virgins for a time
    everyday I pray
    you are for me
    only for ever
    us is the key word

this was not a dream coming true
    this was only me coming home to you
    walking along that special avenue
    taking time off to think along
    stealing time away to that other world
    looking for you the one - our sails unfurled

this was not only a dream coming true
    this was only me breaking away from you
    why must we always be so wrong
    think of the time we must accrue
    tell me your truths tell me your lies
    tell me all you see before your eyes

- coming home

to you my love i dedicate my name
    for you my love i go in search of fame
    for you who means everything to me - you who are my life
    for you i will walk any street - i will suffer pain and strife
    about you i will let no evil word be spoke
    about you i will twirl my web of fate
    it is to you i am dedicated
    it is to you that i send all my love.

- dedication

a love like ours has such a cost
  but a love like ours will never be lost
  we are so young and yet so strong
  please lord let nothing go wrong

when the cat is away will the mouse play?
  let us be founded upon a mutual trust
  people are against us - they say we will go bust
  we know what we want and will keep it

a love like ours has such a cost
  but a love like ours will never be lost
  we are so young and yet so strong
  please lord let nothing go wrong

remember if it were not for you i would've left this mixed fruit
  your future is my future and so i stay to see you through
  dream your dream for me and i'll dream my dream for you
  we know what we want and will get it

a love like ours has such a cost
  but a love like ours will never be lost
  we are so young and yet so strong
  please lord let nothing go wrong
  there are a million lonely people in the world
  we have each other - we have a guiding light
  it may not be visible continuously but it burns with all its might
  we know what we want and can see it

a love like ours has such a cost
  but a love like ours will never be lost

we are so young and yet so strong
please lord let nothing go wrong

we must live by a code of trust
trust in ourselves - trust in each other
and in no other man or his brother
we know what we want and will never regret it

walking the high wire
on one side is love
on the other sadness
rising with the dawn dew
into a clear sky
can you want me?
will you take me?
but wait the rope is taut
it snaps
i fall but
not into oblivion
i am tumbling down the love chute
away from peril
getting nearer to you

i have lied for it
    i have cried over it
    i nearly died because of it

oh! what an ill-gotten gain
    foreboding and treacherous - the little man warns of trust
    walking in the rain
    the vortex is born in lust

looks power and riches - a package deal
    yet you have so much to give and so little to steal
    again i dwell on trust but it has soon left
    my hand lingers between your cleft

a laugh a smile but is it all worthwhile?
    we have waited so long - things are going strong
    the risk I take please don't let it be a fake
    does she know how I feel my mind is a reel

i have lied for it
    i have cried over it
    i nearly died because of it

- *love*

i woke up to a sinking sun
    i'd met a false friend
    what could i do but run
    the colour of the sky the smell of the sea
    rain odours warning sticky times waiting at bay
    what could a man want but she

you came into my life with the rising orb
    gone to the wind a breath of adrenalin
    birds in a tree looking at me
    fear in their eyes yet a pumping love in their breasts
    looking hard and fast you began to smile
    it was time open the night file

a fast breath a quick laugh
    you began to grow inside me
    a parasitic symbol was born
    arms around your neck a scarf
    i began to grow in you
    a spark touched two stones opposing

yet momentarily coagulating a glimmer of life

the gate to life children of him

the glimmering light began to shimmer
    the heat from our bodies a source of constant warmth
    little could stop it the avalanche had begun
    white love cells being borne a million doves in flight

a viewpoint on the individual
fly on the old prison wall
what appall

the time has begun my boy
    to lay down your gun
    lay it down in the dust
    the dust of a thousand men
    their rotting corpses
    wasted away to nothing
    from nothing in the noon day sun
    my boy the time has come

when the dust settles
    and you see
    into the distance
    black clouds looming
    do not search out your gun
    my boy for your time has come
    to join the storm
    to rain with those clouds
    to make the dust settle
    for good in the mud
    of creation

- *hope for the future*

tune
  into life
  at home
  and someday
  your children
  will buy
  the romanticism
  of your memories
  on some technology disc
  while you hobble
  through life
  marred
  by the shell
  guided in
  by the sound
  of your
  little link
  with life
  in the real world

wake up you are dreaming sweet one
    it's really a nice day out somewhere
    we were moving away from the border
    i opened my eyes and from the depth of her heart
    i was blinded by purity
    yet no-one had told her about the pain involved
    it's always a rainy day when you are not around

oh babe what have they done this time
    come with me and stay with me please stay she pleads
    yet the dust creeps into my shell
    eating at what little emotion still exists
    don't point a finger at me love inside I am a runaway
    they say that only the dead go free - someone shoot us
    i just cower in the corner and wait

sinking into submission they took me away
    and now i see the wire that suffocates my spirit
    a criminal is punished and then set free
    we are sentenced for speaking out
    caught between what's sure and all this violence
    madness lingers on my brow and i sigh
    but soon babe our spirits can soar and we'll be free

copper-pink blush in a dawn sky
    crisp freshness of a new day
    silver lit trees let my mind fly
    red-faced goblins on a moonlit pathway

my head spins round and round
    eyes focused on a vision
    military regime pins me to the ground
    soon I shall willingly return to prison

green grass tickles - soft sunlight soothes
    acorns massaging my back
    it is so simple to sink into these grooves
    people so open - getting away with the flock

colours splashed across the country
    racialism drowning in its own blood
    subconsciously soothed by the sultry
    to be drowned again by the flood

infusion of our shadowy shapes
    thoughts lost in the labyrinth of the fire
    how sweet the pure air tastes
    it feels so good to be out of the quagmire

yellow tinged boat - cigarette butt in a ten minute stream
    floating aimlessly through the channels of his mind
    thunderstorm crashing the windows of his dream
    huddled over his brown bottle
    you got to be cruel to be kind

bright lights twinkling on a sea of green
    christmas feeling hanging on the air
    why the exile where has he been
    depression cracking his face
    i'm not there

pillars of salt ready to crumble
    so fragile under the hawk eyes of their so-called superiors
    they stood erect - clean shaven short hair
    symbols of a hygienic system
    yet their feet drowned in their sweating boots
    while the flies laid eggs in their ears

yellow orb new to a virgin sky
    cloudless day yet cloud filled minds
    nervous tension cracking a perfect day
    square beds square people - establishment
    dust to polish to dust a vicious circle
    inspection time again

nurturing and developing
    the killer instinct
    dark and bloody
    but red red
    can you believe it!
    before it is burnt
    black then dark
    dark as swollen rivers
    once your looming clouds
    have split - figlike
    revealing their tender vulvas -
    rivers that were lucid
    but now grumble a dark brown
    laced with soil
    you avidly claim yours
    soil that passing
    emerges black
    the only difference
    mine is recycled
    yours slushes onto the pile

sometime my friend
     you will see
     that all is not
     what is meant to be
     and then
     you will come
     crawling to me
     in search of your
     freedom

and i will sit
     behind your chains
     dreaming of a life
     you can never be

so keep on shuffling
     past my window
     until you fall
     to your knees
     and while your eyes fill
     with the truth
     of life
     you will begin
     to crawl to me

onto a blood red sky
   the lune
   sheds a glistening tear
   for our dark continents
   which sag
   beneath countless martyrs
   some long dead
   others cooling
   yet all sacrificed
   to some or other
   lost cause

she stands swirling like
a breath of fresh air
in a dust storm
tingling the sense pads
she batters my brain
with alarm bells
opening my mind
like a long lost
rust hinged door and
placing my self defences
up against
crumbling walls

how singularly sickening
    these diseases of
    the mind that
    eradicate pain and fear
    substituting feelings
    with fanaticism and
    driving men
    to their deaths
    in the name
    of peace

so it is that
    i must wait in
    growing dread for
    the warrant that will
    transport me to
    a line on
    their monument of
    war dead

saga-like the green hands
    twirl through the sweet mist
    pulling him down from
    individuality into the collective
    consciousness

swirling round his eyes roll
    from ogre to ogre a full circle
    of intimacy - worshipping
    the full moon

he moves onto their level
    warm coals glowing
    welling up from his belly
    bursting into his head

the moon passes on clockwise
    until it is tossed
    from the circle
    his rheumy eyes follow
    feeling it land

he sees a mouse
    scurry from its presence
    her eyes glistening yellow
    in its dying embers

About the Author

Author, poet, ethicist and philosopher, Rand Leeb-du Toit, is the author of *Fierce Reinvention, A Guide to Harnessing Your Superpowers for Entrepreneurial and Leadership Success.*

He has been writing poetry all his life. This is his first anthology.

Rand is a heart transplant survivor and lives in Sydney, Australia.

Also by Rand Leeb-du Toit

Non Fiction

Fierce Reinvention